IRON
SELF-DISCIPLINE

DAILY HABITS TO RESIST TEMPTATION AND BUILD
THE WILLPOWER TO ACHIEVE YOUR LONG TERM GOALS

MARKUS A. KASSEL

Table of Contents

Intro: Self-Discipline = the Key to Achieving Dreams?   - 6 -

Part I: Discipline as a Learnable Skill   - 9 -

Part II: Why You May Be Lacking Willpower   - 14 -

01) You Never Learned It   - 14 -

The Problem   - 14 -

What to Do about It   - 15 -

02) You Won't Even Try   - 17 -

The Problem   - 17 -

What to Do about It   - 17 -

03) You Experience Super Strong Cravings   - 18 -

The Problem   - 18 -

What to Do about It   - 19 -

04) You Lack Self-Confidence   - 20 -

The Problem   - 20 -

What to Do about It   - 21 -

05) You Subscribe to Immediate Gratification   - 22 -

The Problem   - 22 -

What to Do about It   - 23 -

06) You Have to Deal with Emotional Stress   - 23 -

The Problem   - 23 -

What to Do about It .... - 24 -

Part III: So What? Or Why You Need to Address Your Lack of Self-Discipline ASAP .... - 26 -

    Never Reaching Any of Your Goals .... - 27 -

    Poor Impulse Control .... - 28 -

    Substance Abuse Problems .... - 28 -

    Weight Gain & Health Issues .... - 28 -

    Financial Issues .... - 29 -

Part IV: How to Develop Iron-Clad Self-Discipline .... - 30 -

    Define Your Goals .... - 30 -

    Start Practicing .... - 31 -

    Get in Detox-Mode .... - 32 -

    Avoid Temptations (Most of the Time Anyway) .... - 33 -

    Rewire Your Brain .... - 35 -

Part V: Iron-Clad Self-Discipline Applied to Real-Life Situations .... - 37 -

    Define Your Goals .... - 37 -

    Figure Out What You Want .... - 37 -

    SMART It .... - 38 -

    Break It Down .... - 41 -

    Start Practicing .... - 42 -

    Start Small .... - 42 -

Get Organized - 43 -

Get in Detox-Mode - 44 -

Beating Nicotine - 44 -

Overcoming Sugar Cravings - 47 -

Easing Off on the Caffeine - 50 -

Avoid Temptations (Most of the Time Anyway) - 54 -

Cleanse Your Environment - 54 -

Keep It Clean - 55 -

Plan Your Cheat Meals - 58 -

Rewire Your Brain - 60 -

Just Do It, Consistently - 60 -

Part VI: Don't Ever Turn Back by Avoiding Those Common Pitfalls - 65 -

Holidays & Vacations - 65 -

Plan Your Indulgences - 65 -

Super-Size Me, Not! - 66 -

Keep Working Out - 66 -

Dealing with Illness or Injury - 68 -

Give Yourself a Break - 68 -

Remember Your Goals - 68 -

Make a Plan - 69 -

Busy Times at Work - 72 -

Take Some Me-Time   - 72 -

Conclusion: the Beginning of Your Journey   - 74 -

Want to Reach Your Full Potential?   - 76 -

Let's Keep In Touch   - 77 -

About the Author   - 79 -

Intro: Self-Discipline = the Key to Achieving Dreams?

Of all the experiments on self-discipline ever devised, the "Stanford Marshmallow Test" stands as the most famous without a shadow of a doubt.

You probably heard about it on day-1 of your *Intro to Psychology* class (because, yes, it's that basic.) But if you never took psych or aren't really into marshmallows, the experiment is pretty easy to grasp anyway.

Psychologist Walter Mischel and his team would place a single marshmallow in front of a child. The subject was told that he or she could eat the one marshmallow right away or be given two marshmallows if they could wait until the researcher came back into the room. The said researcher would then leave the kid alone with the marshmallow for a few minutes and observe their young subjects' reaction.

Some kids just dug into that one marshmallow, without thinking twice about it, while others attempted to distract themselves from the treat by any means necessary so they could enjoy two later on.

The kids in the second group (the waiters) displayed classic self-discipline. **They delayed gratification in the moment in the hopes of a greater reward down the line**.

The interesting thing about the experiments, though, wasn't how the kids behaved that day (kids want treats, big whoop!), it's what the follow-up research revealed about the subjects years later.

It turns out the kids who exhibited poor impulse control (the marshmallow eaters) did not become as successful as their self-disciplined counterparts, according to a few life metrics like SAT scores, incidence of substance abuse, job success, and even BMI.

Overall, the kids who lacked willpower ended up fatter and dumber than those in control of themselves. I know, that might be simplifying things a little, but it gets the point across: yes, **the kids with higher levels of self-control achieved more fulfilling lives** than the marshmallow eaters.

Self-discipline is a concept that goes way beyond whether you'd like one treat immediately or would be willing to wait to get two. It affects how much effort you put into your daily tasks, how hard you study at school, how you spend your money, how often you indulge in self-destructive behaviors, and whether you'd be ready to put in real work to accomplish your long-term goals.

If you're lacking willpower, you're lacking the ability to live your best life, to realize your dreams and become the person you've always wanted to be.

This book will help you determine why you may be lacking in that department and give you real, concrete ways to start building your willpower, as well as give you tips on avoiding turning back to your old ways once you've begun the journey to iron-clad self-discipline.

If you've made up your mind, take a deep breath, turn the page and let us begin!

Part I: Discipline as a Learnable Skill

Whether you never had it or lost it somewhere along the way, developing your self-discipline can be a difficult skill. But it remains a skill nonetheless.

The kids in the Marshmallow Test proved that some people are just inherently better at controlling their whims and desires than others but that, in no way, means you're stuck with the level of self-discipline you were born with. **Even if you've always been a self-confessed marshmallow eater, you can still repent and turn it around**.

Kelly McGonigal, another Stanford professor exploring the psychology behind self-discipline, has come to the conclusion that willpower is much like a muscle. Think about doing an exhausting high-rep set of biceps curls. With every rep, you fatigue a little more and are slightly less able to perform another with good form. By your last rep, you're struggling so much you may not even be able to finish.

Willpower works the same way.

You keep using it throughout the day, so it gets tired and less able to function properly. That's why, by the end of the day, you may be more likely to give in to food cravings or to let your temper out than in the morning when you hadn't yet worn down your ability to keep yourself in check.

The concept is called ego depletion or, more appropriately, willpower depletion, and it isn't just psychological guesswork.

While it makes sense that your willpower may dwindle the more you ignore or avoid certain situations (just think about how hard it becomes to bite your tongue after hours of listening to some BS you don't agree with), there may be actual biological evidence of willpower depletion.

You don't just get bored of holding off and suddenly decide to shake things up. Research has emerged in the last few years concerning an area of the brain (known as the dorsolateral prefrontal cortex) that would be tied to self-control and making the right decision when presented with several options.

Scientists from the University of Iowa found that the dorsolateral prefrontal cortex becomes less and less active as you progress through a series of tests involving self-discipline. **Your ability to make a smart decision literally lessens as you keep trying to pick the best option**. As if each new choice exerted its toll on your IQ!

Willpower and blood sugar levels also seem to be correlated. In several studies, the subjects who were asked to perform a series of tasks drawing on their self-discipline showed lower blood glucose levels afterward than the control group. Researchers think this may have to do with how much more energy it takes to exercise willpower than to just hang out and not stress about keeping yourself in check.

Because the brain uses glucose as its #1 energy source, **the exhausting mental task of having to resist temptation actually depletes blood glucose at a higher rate**.

Still, the biological evidence for willpower depletion doesn't explain why some people are self-control machines and others only need the slightest push to get them to fall off the willpower wagon and dive face-first into a pan of brownies.

Some researchers suggest it all comes down to your mental attitude toward willpower. Studies have shown that people who believe willpower to be a limited resource, as in the willpower depletion theory, give up on tasks faster than those who think willpower is basically infinite – or can at least be stretched a little bit.

That sounds like you can trick yourself into having stronger self-discipline if you just believe hard enough. There is definitely something to be said for willing things into existence.

Visualization techniques are often recommended to people trying to make a positive change in their lives. However, you don't have to turn your back on the science of willpower depletion in order to change your mindset about self-discipline. Research also shows that your intentions and your attitude go a long way in your willpower struggle.

Doctor Mark Muraven from the University of Albany has posited that a person's motivation plays a big part in whether or not they will complete a self-control task.

Willpower depleted subjects kept trying at a task of self-discipline when told that it would benefit them personally or benefit someone else, while those who were not motivated in the same way gave up more easily.

This is why having your own goals is so important to gaining self-discipline. Wanting something for yourself, rather than doing it because someone else asks you to, could spell the difference between getting it done and just giving up.

You don't run a 5K because someone told you to; you do it because it'll make you feel good or because something is chasing after you and you'd rather not end up as its meal. If you don't want or need to be doing it, you're less likely to finish the task.

Lastly, **your general attitude can also have an impact on your willingness to exercise willpower**.

We've all experienced this first hand. After a long, crappy day that has put you in a bad mood, you're not going to come home and decide to ignore that bottle of whisky in the cabinet. You won't choose that day to start your diet or to quit smoking.

Those bad mood days are more likely to result in you failing to use any self-discipline at all, and resorting to your usual coping mechanisms to make yourself feel better.

On the other hand, when you've had a great day and you're feeling good, you know you'll be more likely to continue that streak and do something that benefits you. Those are the days you head to the gym after work or order a kale & quinoa salad for dinner.

So, to sum it all up, willpower is influenced by both physiological and psychological factors. You could be physically drained of any resolve, but your reasons for carrying out a task (as well as your mood at the time) could still help you muster up the self-discipline necessary to get the job done.

Professor McGonigal (the one from Stanford, not Hogwarts), continuing with her muscle analogy, reveals that – in the same manner – **willpower can be trained and strengthened by using it more often**.

Those tricky high-rep sets we talked about get easier as you develop endurance in your muscles. The same can be said about self-control. The more you exercise it, the better you'll be able to say no to that junk food, not yell at other drivers no matter how idiotic they're being, or go to the gym after work even though you're exhausted and just want to watch TV all night.

Part II: Why You May Be Lacking Willpower

When you think about it, you can't really expect to fix a problem if you ignore where it stems from, right?

So, before we even begin discussing any tip for improving your discipline, **we need to turn our attention inward and explore the reason or reasons why you may be struggling with willpower**.

01) You Never Learned It

The Problem

You've always been given what you want and never really had to discipline yourself. You were probably a super spoiled kid, a popular teenager and a party animal in College.

Not that you were a jerk, unintelligent or unambitious, but stuff kind of just fell into your lap without much work on your part. And now, the concept of having to actually deprive yourself of immediate gratification for the sake of a future goal might seem a little baffling. Your charmed life has come back to bite you in the butt.

Or maybe you never really cared about much anything as a youth and are now just finding your ambition.

Either way, the problem is you never acquired the emotional tools required to reaching goals – simply because you never needed them before!

Now, you're stuck wishing you could accomplish those dreams but not knowing how to proceed.

In other words, you never learned how to control yourself or what it means to exercise self-discipline.

This one is pretty obvious: sorry, but **you'll have to kiss your old EZ life goodbye and start doing some actual work on yourself**.

Don't cry; it won't be that hard. It's not like you were Richie Rich or Mr. Burns anyway, right? You were probably not born with a silver spoon in your mouth. Which means that, at one point or another, you've had to exercise some kind of self-discipline. It may not have been a huge deal at the time but you did do it. You're not completely in unknown territory.

Let that be your model for your future willpower endeavors. Cling onto that one time you can remember that maybe you skipped a party to study or thought you'd rather drive to the bar and be the designated driver instead of getting totally slammed.

You have, on at least one occasion in the past, shown you had willpower, and you can do it again. Believe that "self-disciplined you" is in there, somewhere, and pull the sucker out.

Honestly, setting your mind on becoming a more determined person represents a great first step in acquiring that quality. Intentions lead to actions.

If after rummaging through your brain, you still can't think of any instance where you displayed self-control, pick someone else you admire that often puts aside their immediate desires for the "greater good."

It could be the guy who skips a lot of parties to study, the guy who goes to bed early even though cool stuff is happening. That person will represent the example you want to emulate.

The psychological term for this process is called "modeling." **Imitating someone you esteem is a proven way to change personality traits you need to work on**. Don't start wearing their clothes and duplicating their speech patterns. You don't want to Single White Female your role model. Just act the way they do in a situation in which you envy their skills.

Maybe your friend often stays at home instead of going to the bar because he has work to do in the morning. You're in the same position, except that you – on the other hand – always pick the party over not being hungover.

Not great.

So you want to change your behavior so you can actually function at work the following day and not spend those hours with a sledgehammer banging inside the walls of your skull?

Before you head out, pause for a second and think. Ask yourself how your responsible friend would act in this situation and why they would act that way. Model your behavior after them (modeling! Get it?).

Imitation is the sincerest form of flattery, and also one of the best ways to becoming the person you want to be.

02) You Won't Even Try

The Problem

Controlling yourself is hard, I know! Maybe you tried to tough it out a few times, completely failed, and decided to live the easy life. Maybe hard work just isn't your thing and you never really attempted to exhibit some self-discipline.

No matter which doctrine you subscribe to, when you're faced with a challenge, the end result is the same: you take the path of least resistance because it's easier and more fun.

What to Do about It

JUST GIVE IT A TRY!

It might seem a little counterintuitive that, in order to gain self-discipline, you need self-discipline... but just like with any other skill **you can't get better if you don't practice**.

It's alright to screw up. It's alright to attempt to control yourself and still fail. There's a definite learning curve, but you have to actually attempt to gain willpower if you want to develop some.

Once you start seeing self-discipline as a skill that needs patience and practice, rather than an all-or-nothing state of being, you'll be more likely to stick with it.

Remember you won't just wake up with willpower one day. It's not a superpower you can acquire by being bitten by a particularly in-control radioactive spider. You have to work for it!

Trying and failing is OK, as long as you don't quit. Giving in to every whim without even a hint of an attempt at self-control isn't going to get you very far. Don't give up just because it's hard; don't give into your cravings or your self-destructive behaviors because it's easier.

Try to better yourself. The more you'll try, the better you'll be.

03) You Experience Super Strong Cravings

The Problem

As we've seen, self-discipline is all about denying yourself something you want right now in order to reach your longer-term goals.

You say no to dessert because you want to lose weight; you pass on a smoke break because you're trying to quit; you don't watch one episode of a really great TV show a week because you want to binge the hell out of it all winter.

But **what happens when your cravings are just too strong to deny**?

In certain cases, you might experience disturbing physical symptoms when you're trying to stay the course and say "no". You probably won't withdraw from watching TV so you're pretty safe there, but sugar, caffeine and nicotine cravings are very real, and so are the withdrawal symptoms they can cause.

Trying to cut any of those substances out of your life can lead to headaches, irritability, body pain, nausea, anxiety, trouble sleeping... And unless you're on the masochistic side, you probably won't want to deal with all that!

Not only is it uncomfortable to being with; it's also highly inconvenient to even have to put up with one of those symptoms. **Everyone is way too busy to attempt getting through their to-do list while also feeling like they just got hit by a truck.**

That's why, more often than not, people just give into those cravings. The substance might be bad for you but at least it'll make the symptoms go away and help you get on with your day.

The problem is if you always give into cravings rather than dealing with the discomfort of withdrawal symptoms; you never actually get over needing that substance and it stands in the way of you achieving your goals.

What to Do about It

The best thing you can do when cravings rule your life is to detox from the substance that is giving you those irresistible urges.

Honestly, there's no magic pill to beating cravings. Your only option is getting off the stuff completely. You may whine and fight against the idea of giving up sugar, cigarettes, booze or caffeine, but if those sources of pleasure have become your master and are now infringing on your life in a real, measurable way, it's time to get rid of them once and for all.

It's going to suck; make no mistake about it. The only advice I can give you is to keep your goal in mind. You eventually want to be a nonsmoker or a person who doesn't rely on caffeine to be able to live their life. Through all the crappy withdrawal symptoms, just keep that goal in mind.

If it doesn't happen now, when will it? Will you suddenly become a willpower machine after two more years of smoking like a chimney? It's highly doubtful.

Keep your goal in mind. The time will pass, whether you're detoxing or not, and your time will be much better spent getting healthier and learning some much needed self-discipline.

04) You Lack Self-Confidence

The Problem

In short, self-confidence is your belief in your ability to complete a task successfully. If you don't believe in yourself, you basically have close to zero chance of exercising serious self-discipline.

Willpower relies on your aptitude to be your own cheerleader and follow through with what you said you were going to do (or not do). If you don't even think you can accomplish that, then you're screwed. Big time.

Lack of self-confidence and lack of self-discipline are often closely linked. It's not surprising that someone's low opinion of themselves would translate into an inability or unwillingness to control their behavior in a tempting situation.

It's an "I can't do it anyway, so why try?" kind of situation. The good thing is that beginning to exercise self-discipline can help with your self-confidence overall and keep increasing your belief in your willpower.

If self-confidence is tied to your (perceived) ability to complete any given task, then it stands to reason that it can be built upon by setting and completing challenges. When you show yourself you can do something, you'll come to realize you can do it again. And more.

Start very small. Say no to one dessert, work through one coffee break, skip one trip outside to smoke. **Self-confidence can be built fairly rapidly when you start with tiny tasks**. If you doubt you could refuse a smoke break, just think back to a time when you did.

What do you mean you can't NOT eat that cake? You've been awake for a few hours without eating any piece of it and you're still breathing... So what are a few more hours? Delay and delay, until you either forget about it or pass the chance altogether. Double negatives aside, your self-confidence in your ability to say "no" will increase when you have real world experience of the matter.

The idea is to start small and build off your victories. Your willpower will nurture your self-confidence which will, in turn, increase your willpower some more, and so on, and so on. A beautiful cycle where, once you get the ball rolling, the sky is the limit.

05) You Subscribe to the Culture of Immediate Gratification

The Problem

It's a sad state of affairs but we want everything and we want it right NOW. If you're looking for someone to blame, point a finger at our society which has set up a system of immediate gratification where you can order your coffee ahead of time and pick it up immediately, because who can waste five precious minutes in line?

We've got fast food, online shopping, home delivery of anything you can think of, about five different kinds of instant messaging, and on demand television, podcasts, music, and movies. Whatever you could want, it's no more than a few clicks away.

Except when it comes to stuff that actually takes time and discipline. **You can download the app that will help you learn to play the guitar but you can't purchase the skill**; you still have to put in hours of practice time to even get to beginner level.

In this day and age where immediacy reigns supreme, stuff that takes more than a few minutes is deemed tedious and too difficult to accomplish. So, a lot of people give up. They see that a skill will take longer than expected to obtain, and require much more willpower to master, and they decide it isn't for them after all.

To avoid feeling overwhelmed by the scope of the goal at hand, break it down into manageable chunks that can be completed a little at a time.

Handling the guitar like Jimi Hendrix will seem impossible when you don't even know how to play one chord. So start there; start at the beginning with the darn basics. Learn step by step and don't even think about the larger goal which might intimidate and discourage you rather than inspire you.

Break your huge Hendrix target into smaller, easier to accomplish milestones, and focus on the task at hand. That way, you will actually get that feeling of immediate gratification while still working toward a larger more satisfying goal. Every time you move up a notch, you'll get that rush of gratification and the encouragement to continue to the next level.

06) You Have to Deal with Emotional Stress

The Problem
Indulging in a bad habit or destructive behavior can represent a coping mechanism to deal with emotional turmoil.

Maybe your home or work life is way too stressful to even begin to think about kicking a soothing habit. You indulge to make yourself feel better and end up even deeper down the rabbit hole of that bad habit.

What to Do about It

Recognize that it happens to everyone. Using coping mechanisms during stressful periods is normal and you shouldn't beat yourself up about it.

The problem comes when you use the smallest stresses to justify bad habits. Your house plant dying is not a legitimate excuse to eat an entire carton of ice cream. You don't really care that much. Make sure you're making a legitimate separation between events that just annoy you and issues that are actual reasons to be in distress. Don't be a drama queen.

When something irritates you (without crossing into affliction territory), you know deep down you don't need to resort to that destructive coping mechanism to make yourself feel better. So, hold off for ten minutes, take a walk, watch a cat-themed YouTube video or whatever. Your anger will subside and you'll feel less likely to ruin yourself with some destructive habit.

Times of actual distress are a little different.

Overeating, binge drinking, drug use and otherwise harmful behaviors are common during these hard periods. When you're going through a rough patch, it may be a good idea to replace your habitual, deleterious reactions with a different, more positive one. Or at least try to.

Easier said than done, when you know that thing would make you feel better immediately. Remind yourself that your coping mechanism is:

a) Probably killing you;

b) Your default response when you ought to face a delicate and nerve-racking situation.

So, if you want to feel less tense AND still be alive, you'll need to find a new way to relieve that pressure. Proven long-term stress-relief techniques include exercise of basically any kind, meditation and journaling.

Start any (or all) of these positive activities and you'll begin to feel more serene and able to deal with the harsh obstacles that come your way in the future.

Lessening stress in your everyday world is key to creating effective long-term healthy coping mechanisms.

Part III: So What? Or Why You Need to Address Your Lack of Self-Discipline ASAP

In your day-to-day life, self-discipline may be the last thing on your mind. If you're going through a stressful period, have to deal with a busy schedule or all your TV shows are getting really darn good, you'll want to skip the willpower moments and just indulge.

You're thinking: "I've had a stressful day, so I deserve my six-pack of beer, full bag of chips..." or whatever your preferred poison is. Now, I've said it before, treating yourself can be a good thing; we all need indulgences to keep ourselves sane and on track to meet our ultimate goals. But **there's a danger lurking behind those *treat yourself* moments**.

The rationale is that it's *just once*. You're giving yourself a treat after this *one* stressful day, and tomorrow you'll start your diet and exercise plan or you'll use your after work time to learn that skill you've been telling yourself you'd catch up on.

But let's be honest; if you actually look at all the 'just this once' moments in any given month, you'll most likely find that your treats aren't so much treats as daily habits explained away by a false idea that you only do your destructive habits once in a while. That's why you should be at least trying to exercise your willpower every day; so your "once in a whiles" don't turn into "every days" without your knowledge.

If you're still thinking: "so what? A lifetime of treating yourself sounds pretty awesome to me", just consider what will be the result of such a behavior. This daily lack of self-control can lead to some pretty intense consequences down the line.

Never Reaching Any of Your Goals

Maybe right now, in this moment, you're fine with drinking all night, every night. I mean, it's pretty fun, yeah. But when does it end? What are your long term goals? Where do you want to be in 5 years? Will constantly treating yourself help you get there?

Unless you want to be the oldest, least accomplished guy at the frat party, I highly doubt an indulgent lifestyle will get you where you want to be. Not working on your willpower leads to an inability to set and reach even the most basic of goals. You procrastinate doing the smallest tasks, like washing the dishes, because they aren't fun and aren't life-threateningly urgent.

You don't give up what you want now (i.e. time to chill out) for something that will benefit you in the long run. This leads to a stagnant life of never wanting to set goals and never having the ability to achieve them anyway.

Poor Impulse Control
In Part I, we talked about willpower being like a muscle; getting stronger the more you use it. Well, the analogy works both ways.

If you lay in bed all day for months, your muscles will start to atrophy. You'll get weak. Similarly, **if you give in to every temptation that comes your way** (aka not using an ounce of self-control) **your willpower will weaken even more**, until you may even be physically unable to resist things. Being super impulsive and indulgent all the time can lead to serious consequences in every aspect of your life.

Substance Abuse Problems
The kids in the Stanford Marshmallow Test that showed poor impulse control actually had a higher instance of substance abuse issues.

It makes sense when you think about it. Addiction to drugs, alcohol, nicotine or even caffeine doesn't come from a one-time indulgence. It comes from being unable to resist the cravings for the substance, indulging way too frequently, and coming to depend on the substance for a feeling of normalcy. If you have poor impulse control, you're just more likely to give in to a substance craving than if you had a good grasp on your willpower.

Weight Gain & Health Issues
Again, it makes sense that someone without willpower would gain weight quicker than someone with good impulse

control and self-discipline. Do they want seconds? Nope. Does Mr. No Willpower? Probably. Ditto dessert.

But weight gain will be the least of your problems if you can't say "no" to junk food and "yes" to a workout. If you're constantly living that indulgence life, your health could go south pretty fast. You might be looking at diabetes, metabolic syndrome, depression, anxiety, heart conditions, insomnia, heartburn and digestive issues. If you can't will yourself to make healthy choices, your health will decline.

Financial Issues
People with self-control issues will either not have a budget or have pretty hard time sticking to one. They're easily swayed by their impulses and sweet discounts on stuff they don't even need.

Rather than exercising willpower, researching your options, and saving up for stuff you want, you find yourself buying a bunch of useless crap and making poor investments. You may end up with a kickass dinosaur-shaped bouncy castle in your apartment but you'll also have to deal with a big hole in your wallet.

Part IV: How to Develop Iron-Clad Self-Discipline

Define Your Goals

If you have nothing to work toward, then the work of self-discipline may seem useless. You'll find yourself thinking, "Why the heck am I resisting this temptation?" because there will be no greater reason for your willpower than just depriving yourself of what you want right then and there.

If you have a goal, something you really want to achieve, however, exercising willpower starts to have a purpose beyond just making you miserable. When everything you do is either another step toward your goal or a step in the opposite direction, self-discipline becomes an invaluable tool for growth and progress.

Of course, goal setting itself requires a little reflection and self-discipline. Where are you now, compared to where you want to be? What can you do to move toward that desired version of yourself? Are you truly willing to do what it takes to get there?

Remember that achieving goals doesn't have to suck. Improving yourself is not meant to make you sad and depressed. Don't set goals you don't actually want to achieve just because they sound good. A shocking number of people say their ultimate goal is to run a marathon, even though they hate running and would rather cut their legs off than train for the run.

Goals don't need to sound good to other people. You're not improving your life for them; you're doing it for you! So, set a goal you actually want to achieve and one you'll enjoy working toward. It won't always be easy, but it should at least be worthwhile to you.

Don't spend your time and energy turning yourself into a clone or someone you don't like. That would be the ultimate tragedy.

Start Practicing

As we've seen earlier, willpower is a skill. You aren't born with it and you don't just stumble upon it. You work for it by putting in some effort every single day.

It doesn't even have to be a lot of effort. You don't have to start by sitting down and completing a 2,000 piece puzzle in one sitting or attempting to read *War and Peace* by next week.

Start small. Finish little tasks.

Fold your laundry, put the dishes away, finally organize your record collection; tiny tasks that are easy to complete, albeit super boring, and very tempting to quit.

It's by completing these little annoying chores that your willpower will begin to grow. A lot of the time, achieving goals involves a little bit of doing stuff you don't want to do. You may enjoy 95% of acquiring a new skill, but there will certainly be something about it you want to put off; one thing you just can't stand about the process.

And this is where pushing through and being willing and able to finish mundane tasks will really come in handy. When you're willing to put in the boring work for the greater reward, you'll start to become a master of willpower.

Get in Detox-Mode

Bad habits can just come down to addiction or physical dependence. We tend to think of addiction as a super-intense life-ruining disease that we would know if we had.

You're not shooting heroin in an abandoned Baltimore row house like a character on *The Wire,* so you can't possibly be an addict, right? Well, not really.

Studies have shown that sugar lights up the same pleasure centers in the human brain as cocaine and heroin. It can also cause the same cravings associated with hard drug use and similar withdrawal symptoms. Yikes. So **sugar is basically a drug, and if you're addicted to it you won't be resisting it anytime soon, no matter how much willpower you think you have**.

Of course, sugar isn't the only substance you could be addicted to that could be messing with your willpower. You'll want to detox from whatever it is you can't resist. Exercising willpower over something potentially addictive is much easier when you're no longer addicted to it. You'll be starting from a much healthier place and be much more willing and able to resist the temptation once you've rewired your body to not crave it anymore.

Nobody is saying it'll be easy, but getting out from under that addiction will do wonders for your health and really help you rev up your willpower.

Avoid Temptations (Most of the Time Anyway)

A lot of the time, when you're trying to will yourself not to do something, you just have to keep that temptation away from you.

Not that it's necessarily as simple as that, but straight up avoiding temptation can be really useful in getting yourself on track. Even if the thing you're trying to avoid is all you think about during your time away from it, you're still making progress if you can manage to keep your distances.

You could be sitting there, gritting your teeth, clenching your fists until they're white and praying a Twinkie truck crashes outside your house, but if you don't actually give in to that sugar craving it's a total win, and you're one step closer to kicking the habit altogether.

So, don't keep your downfall in your darn house! If you tend to binge on a certain junk food, don't have it easily accessible, just hanging out in your cupboard. It will start to call your name, and it's a lot harder to hear it from the store shelf than from your kitchen.

Similarly, if you always convince yourself you'll just go for one drink at happy hour but always, without fail, end up drunk off doing 90s R&B karaoke in Koreatown, maybe you could stand to skip the after work drink party once in a while.

Basically, avoid the substances and situations that you know aren't doing you any favors. You can't eat a whole box of Twinkies if they're not there, and you can't drink 8 pints and serenade the karaoke bar with the sweet sounds of Boyz II Men if you're not there.

That being said, you don't actually have to avoid temptation 24/7. If the theory is true and each time we use our willpower it weakens just a little bit, **you may want to pick your battles**.

We start the day avoiding donuts and not giving our superiors any sass back, but all those instances deplete our self-discipline reserves and chip away at the wall that's holding back our temper or willingness to forgo sweet stuff in favor of something healthy. Exercising self-discipline is great but, sometimes, getting to your breaking point isn't worth it. Treating yourself with the occasional indulgence will help keep those floodgates closed.

That's why the concept of a cheat meal in the fitness world was invented. You work out and eat clean 6.5 days out of the week, and use 1 meal to eat what you weren't able to the rest of the week. Knowing the cheat is coming makes sticking to your plan for the rest of the week much easier. It's not "never again"; it's just "later".

It's also a good idea to occasionally give into temptation when you're trying to kick a habit because going cold turkey can totally backfire. If you completely avoid something until you think you're over it, then reintroduce it somehow, you might be looking at a serious relapse. You haven't learned how to avoid that thing in a healthy way; you just ignore it.

So when you've gone 3 months without sugar and decide to indulge in some birthday cake, you'll probably realize how amazing sugar actually is, how much you missed it, and how easily you could be eating it all the time. Then you do. All the time. And you're back to square one.

Little indulgences help you stay on track and make sure the ban is willpower based, and not an unhealthy mental block.

Rewire Your Brain

The old, purely anecdotal, school of thought was that it took 21 days to form a new habit. This came from observations in the 1950s by plastic surgeon Dr. Maxwell Maltz. He observed that his patients took an average of 21 days to get used to whatever new look Maltz had given them. People took that number as gospel for quite some time, not really caring to question its legitimacy.

I don't know why people thought getting used to a new nose and forming a new habit were related but whatever. In 2010, a study was undertaken to figure out what the actual timeframe was for developing a new habit. The answer turned out to be about 2 months, not 3 weeks.

This number also varied widely depending on the person, and the task that they were attempting to make routine. It took some people up to 8 months to actually create an automatic habit. That's 8 months of reminding yourself every day to perform this task. Eight months of "Wasn't there something I was supposed to do today? Oh, damnit! Right. I have to floss".

The upshot is that you have to give it time. Don't rely on the outdated 21-days-to-a-new-habit statistic. If it happens in 21 days, then more power to you, but don't get discouraged if it doesn't. And if you've already attempted something for 3 weeks and gave up after it didn't stick, try again. Sure, three weeks sounds a lot easier than 8 months, but 8 months out of the entire rest of your life is still a drop in the bucket. It's more than worth the investment to change your life for the better.

Also, take into account that your mental attitude toward self-discipline plays a part in whether or not you'll actually be able to stick to something.

Belief in your ability to exercise your own willpower actually increases your willpower; as does your attitude. Being happy and positive increases your ability to flex that self-discipline muscle. Not that it's easy to always be in a good mood, but positivity can be cultivated at any point.

A simple "I can do this" or even "I want to be able to eventually do this" can go a long way in getting your mind to the right place to want to exercise willpower.

Part V: Iron-Clad Self-Discipline Applied to Real-Life Situations

If it all still sounds a little too theoretical, this section will give you step-by-step guides for how to apply the tips outlined in Part IV to your everyday life.

It'll help you start to develop a willpower plan, and give you the tools needed to put that plan into action.

Define Your Goals

Figure Out What You Want

Sometimes, people get so used to underperforming and playing it safe that they don't even know what their ultimate goal is.

They never think about what they truly want because they know, whatever it is, it'll require a lot of work to get and they're really just not up for trying. So first, put aside the fear of hard work, the fear of failure and all your *I can'ts,* and just think about what you want for your future.

I don't mean what you want to eat for lunch or what show you'll binge watch on Netflix this weekend. We're talking big picture here. **What is your ideal future? The first step in acquiring self-discipline is having something to be disciplined for.** Hard work is much easier when there's a reason you're doing it.

Really think about it. Take some serious you-time and come up with a goal for every part of your life: social, romantic, personal, career, and any other significant aspect of your being.

SMART It

If you've ever been to a personal trainer to set physical goals or participated in a business course about corporate goal setting, you've most likely encountered the SMART system.

It exists in such wildly different realms as physical fitness and business growth because it really works across most disciplines. Growth can happen in all aspects of life and it's really nice to know there's one tried and true goal setting system you can use for all of them.

So what is it? **SMART stands for specific, measurable, attainable, realistic, and time-bound**.

Specific means you should avoid making vague claims. "I want to lose weight" could be a goal, and it's a good start, but it's not exactly painting a picture. There are still questions that need to be answered. Let's take this jumping off point and make it a little more understandable.

The next letter, M for *measurable*, will help with that. A measurable goal has a number attached to it. It answers "how much?" and "by when?" It helps make your goal more concrete and more understandable. Let's say you want to lose 50 pounds. Now your vague, abstract goal of wanting to "lose weight" is coming into focus.

Measurable is also tied to the last letter in the SMART system, T for *time-bound*. Attaching a time frame to your goal is another important component of goal setting. It not only makes your goal more specific and measurable, it also informs the last two components of SMART.

The next two letters, A for *attainable*, and R for *reasonable*, revolve around whether a person can achieve something, and whether you, as an individual, will meet that target.

Is going to the moon technically achievable? If you don't listen to the conspiracy theorists then yes, it's totally achievable. Is it reasonable to think that you will become an astronaut? If you aren't one already then, no offense, but probably not. The difference between a thing being possible and a thing being possible *for you* is pretty staggering when you think about it in astronaut terms. Sometimes, what is a walk in the park for someone can be a trip to the moon for another.

Choose your goals according to what is possible in the real world, and what is possible for you. Is losing 50 pounds possible? Sure. Possible for you? Maybe.

This is where you can come back to the T in your goal and tweak it to reflect the possibilities. If you've decided you want to lose 50 pounds, then start to craft a timeline. Will you be able to do it in 3 weeks? Definitely not. 3 months? Probably not. A loss like that will most likely take about 6 months to a year, depending on your level of commitment.

So, again, you go back to the R in your goal and tweak it to reflect your abilities. How many times a week can you get to the gym? Are you a regular healthy eater? Lay out a reasonable plan that will help you reach your goal within your desired time frame.

You see how all the letters play off each other? Putting it all together, let's say you want to lose 50 pounds in a year. This goal is reasonable for any given human being, and reasonable for you as an individual because you've changed your eating habits and have vowed to go to the gym 3-4 times a week.

There's your goal! *I plan to lose 50 pounds by this time next year by continuing to eat healthy and by working out 3-4 times per week.*

It's specific, it's measurable, it has a deadline attached to it, and it's both possible and reasonable for you as an individual.

You can apply the same practice to any goal. Say you want to save enough money for an all-inclusive trip to Cuba by next winter. Is it measurable? You know how much you have to save by what date, so yes. Is it attainable? Someone out there could do that, so yes. Is it reasonable? That's where the self-reflection comes in. You'll have to look at your income, spending habits and debts to know for sure whether you can potentially save that much money by that time. Then you make it specific by implementing a plan.

"I want to save *$xxx* by *this date* by implementing *these money saving tactics*."

Bam! Another SMART goal.

Break It Down

Large goals are scary and, let's face it, kind of easy to give up on. The idea of bringing the bigger picture to life may seem so huge and so far away that it doesn't even seem possible.

You tell yourself that bailing out on impossible goals is fine; smart even! And suddenly, you've thrown in the towel before you even began. But **very little in life is actually impossible**. Most things just come down to goal setting and hard work. If you've followed the SMART goals steps and you've got yourself a sweet, manageable, attainable goal, start breaking that goal down into smaller steps.

Going with the above example, if you want to lose 50 pounds by this time next year where do you start? Probably with losing the first pound, right?

There's a saying in the fitness community that you don't lose X amount of pounds, you lose one pound X amount of times. A huge number like 50 pounds can be too intimidating to get you to even move your butt. But one pound? One is easy. So figure out what losing that one pound entails, focus on that until it happens, then do it forty-nine more times.

That logic bleeds into every other goal you could possibly have, too. You have to start with the smallest step forward you can make, then just keep continuing to the next. Everything is less overwhelming when broken down into smaller parts.

Start Practicing

There's a lot of talk in this book about self-discipline being a skill that you can practice and master. But if you need some willpower in the first place to gain greater willpower, you can feel stuck at square one.

It's a bit like that saying "you have to spend money to make money", but what if you don't have any dough to begin with? **How do you use something you don't have?**

Start Small

First of all, recognize that on a scale of 0 to 100 your willpower is probably not an irremediable zero.

You may say you completely lack self-discipline so that you'll have an excuse when you go wild on a Sunday night or max out your credit card buying tacos. Yet, if you actually think about it, you'll find that you didn't do any of that because you couldn't stop yourself; you just did it because you felt like it!

That's where you can start exercising some willpower. Feel like you want to do something outrageous that is probably going to be bad for you in the long run? Then, don't do it. Start by not having that last shot at the bar that will almost certainly overdraw your bank account and make it so you can't get out of bed the next day.

It's not a huge sacrifice to not have an extra shot; it's just a small flex of your willpower. Pass by the soda machine at lunch. Don't buy something completely unnecessary. Give up one tiny thing per day you would normally indulge in.

You'll begin to build your confidence in your ability to give things up. You'll start to realize that giving up one or two little indulgences here and there isn't the end of the world. It may not even be difficult. Your old excuse of "I have no willpower" goes completely out the window when you start to do these little flexes.

When you can no longer even convince yourself that you're powerless against your whims, you can start to build up your willpower. All it takes is giving up one thing per day. Not a huge price to pay to increase your self-discipline, is it?

Get Organized

Practicing willpower can be as simple as getting a to-do list down on paper. I think everyone can relate to going to bed with a full to-do list, convincing yourself you'll get it all done tomorrow, just to make the same promise again the next night.

For some reason, we all tend to believe Tomorrow Us will be much more productive than Today Us. Accept that They won't be and you'll be in a much better mindset to start practicing your willpower today.

You don't have to complete your full to-do list. After all, if you're a willpower-lacker, you might have a list a mile long. There are a few strategies people employ when trying to finish a list. Some people like to start with the tasks they want to do the least (the famous "frog to eat" of Brian Tracy.) That way, by the time you've done them, the worst is already over and the rest of the list gets easier and easier. You could also pick one urgent thing and two smaller, less urgent to get done each day. It's not overwhelming, but you will still feel accomplished.

However you decide to go ahead, the important thing is that you get organized. To-do lists, diaries, journals, household chalkboards, a fridge full of Post-It notes, a trained parrot that recites the things you still need to do, whatever works for you, get an organization system happening.

Create a system for yourself and get that stuff done!

Get in Detox-Mode

Crazy cravings for stuff that isn't good for you are huge willpower busters. Taking action and kicking the habit, whatever it may be, can represent the first step in cracking your ability to control yourself wide open.

No craving, no problem!

If you kick a bad habit, you'll not only become mentally stronger because you're not relying on a substance anymore, you'll also have learned some useful self-discipline skills you can transfer to different aspects of your life.

Beating Nicotine

Quitting smoking may be one of the hardest things you ever do. Nicotine is highly addictive. Using it floods your brain with dopamine, the feel-good chemical that gets you hooked and keeps you coming back for more.

Withdrawal symptoms are intense, but the good news is they're usually short lived and manageable. You also begin to reap the benefits of quitting within 20 minutes, so you don't have to wait that long to know that quitting is doing you some good. After just a day, your risk of heart disease begins to decrease, and your blood pressure and heart rate return more or less to normal. You might start to feel pretty awesome in the first few days. Then you might start to feel a little funky.

Don't let this throw you.

Give It 4 Days

Studies show that nicotine withdrawal symptoms are at their worst in most people on the third day of quitting.

This is because the nicotine from your last cigarette, 3 days ago, is finally out of your system and you're really beginning your smoke-free life. Your body is kind of freaking out. It has probably been a while since it's been totally nicotine free and it is desperately in search of normalcy.

This is a pivotal point in the quitting process. Some people get here and think "If I feel this bad after 3 days, I don't want to see what day 4 will feel like!" They think the worst day should have been the first and don't realize that what they're experiencing right then is going to be the worst of it.

So give it 4 days.

Just knowing when the worst of your symptoms will show up can be helpful. You'll still feel like garbage, don't get me wrong, but at least you'll expect it.

Reward yourself on this day. You've made it to the worst part and you deserve a little treat to make it through. Just make sure that treat isn't a cigarette. You can expect milder withdrawal symptoms for up to 2 weeks after this point. Remember that every time you say no to a smoke, you're strengthening your self-discipline muscle and getting closer to being a non-smoker.

Change Your Response to Triggers

For most people, an activity and a cigarette go hand in hand. You smoke while having your morning coffee, you smoke when you're driving to work, you get a call and you light up as if the ring is some sort of Pavlovian signal forcing you to smoke.

It's an automatic response to a given situation. You can't avoid these situations, so you have to change your response to them. Do something else when you're in a situation where you would usually smoke. Chew some gum, take a walk, write down the reasons you're quitting in the first place. Find something that works for you and do that instead. You'll start to rewire your brain to do this other automatic habit.

The same goes for random cravings that aren't tied to a situation. No doubt you'll just be sitting there minding your own business and a strong desire to smoke will come along and bother you. How rude. These strong cravings only last about 30 seconds to a few minutes, then they'll start to subside. The key is to distract yourself for that time.

Do something that requires concentration so the time will go by faster; read something, do a puzzle, try to list the state capitals. Concentrating on something else instead of just sitting there waiting for the craving to subside will make it easier to deal with.

Overcoming Sugar Cravings

By now, you should have realized that for some people sugar can be as addictive as cocaine and, of course, a lot more accessible. It sounds crazy but it's not totally untrue.

Studies have indeed shown that sugar does light up the same parts of the brain as most recreational drugs. Of course, detoxing from a hard street drug is probably a lot worse than getting sugar out of your system. They do share a few symptoms, though. Fatigue, anxiety, body aches, cravings, and headaches are all signs you can expect when detoxing. It might be unpleasant but it is possible, and recommended, to get off the sweet stuff (or at least reduce your intake).

A lot of experts on sugar detoxification don't recommend the gradual weaning strategy, where you eat less and less sugar each day. This strategy can also involve eating a certain amount of sugar per day, and stopping once you've reached your quota. I think you can see the problem with that. You actually have to stop. Your whole issue to begin with is that you don't have the discipline to stop yourself from gorging on chocolate and the likes, and this method wants you to just have a little, then stop.

Not really going to happen, is it?

Full on, cold turkey style sugar detox will probably have you experiencing some gnarly, uncomfortable symptoms, but after it's done you'll be a different person. Your taste buds actually change when you quit sugar. Every time you ingest something sugary after your detox, it'll seem way too sweet. Just like if you give up alcohol for an extended period, then drink one beer. You'll feel the effects of the alcohol a lot sooner than you did before. Your tolerance for sugar will have lowered so much that what you normally used to eat will probably make your teeth hurt just thinking about it.

And that's a good thing!

The slowly-eating-less-and-less-junk system still has you eating junk. How exactly is that a detox? The idea is to get off the stuff totally. Plus, you're way more likely to overeat by accident if you're allowed a little bit of something. It's better to go cold turkey, take the rough withdrawal symptoms for a week or two, and never crave sugar the same way again.

Avoid Artificial Sugars
One important tip during this time is to avoid artificial sweeteners altogether. You may think you're getting all the sweet with none of the side-effects but, because they're zero-calorie, artificial sweeteners mess with your system.

You see, when you're tasting sweet, your body assumes it's about to receive the influx of calories that usually follows the ingestion of sugars. Except that, this time, there won't be any.

What happens then? Well, you guessed it: your sugar cravings will get worse as your body is now looking to get that energy boost it was promised!

Opt for foods with natural sugars instead, like fruits. I know, replacing your pack of sugar-free Oreos with an apple may seem like a really poor substitute, like when they replace an actor on a TV show and expect nobody to notice... But natural sugars will always represent the superior option. You won't be tricking your body into intensifying your sugar cravings, and you'll get the added benefit of fiber and nutrients.

Get Your Sleep Under Control

Make sure to get a lot of sleep while you're weaning yourself off sugar. When you're lacking sleep, your hunger hormone (ghrelin) is released in larger quantities while the satiety hormone (leptin) decreases.

Basically, **when you're sleepy, you're hungrier than ever**.

And to add insult to injury, because you're tired, you're even more likely to crave sugar for a quicker energy boost. If you're already coming down off sugar, the last thing you need is your hormones working against you.

Aim for eight hours of sleep a night to keep that witch ghrelin at bay. Not to mention that you won't be craving anything when you're asleep.

Not that you should sleep your problems away, but if there's a choice between fighting with every fiber of your being against the urge to walk to the convenience store for a Kit-Kat and just dreaming of the Land of Chocolate, you're better off in the dream.

Easing Off on the Caffeine

Have you reached the point where you can't get out of bed without the promise of that jolt of energy? Can't function without a constant stream of java in your system? Is your bloodstream mostly coffee at this point?

If you answered yes to any of those questions, it's probably time to detox. Too much caffeine can lead to anxiety, insomnia, increased heart rate, restlessness and sometimes even nausea.

Getting off caffeine might be one of the hardest willpower challenges because over-caffeination is pretty acceptable in our society. It's not like you're doing drugs, right? If you're overworked and underproductive, you're told to caffeinate, rather than take a break or get a good night's sleep.

You can't avoid the breakfast meeting, coffee break, stay-up-late-and-finish-your-work-at-any-cost culture we live in, so your self-discipline is going to have to be through the roof. Whether you decide to go cold turkey or gradually wean yourself off caffeine, there are some strategies you can use to ease the pain of passing by a Starbucks.

Going Cold Turkey

If you decide to cut your intake from ten cups a day to zero overnight, you're going to feel it. There are no two ways about it.

You could be looking at symptoms, starting between one and three days of stopping, and lasting up to two weeks, depending on your level of intake. These symptoms include the likes of shaking, nausea, trouble sleeping, irritability and headaches.

Don't get too freaked out though. A two week withdrawal is pretty rare. Most people are probably only going to experience the worst symptoms for about two days. If you're planning on going cold turkey, most experts suggest doing it on the weekend or during a holiday, so you don't mess up your productivity at work or take your irritability out on your co-workers.

Bring a Water Bottle Everywhere You Go

Staying hydrated is your first line of defense against any caffeine withdrawal symptoms you might experience while you detox.

It also gives you an excuse to refuse a caffeinated drink at a meeting or a friend's place, and gives you something to mindlessly sip on while you work.

Sometimes, it's just the habit of the bad behavior that keeps the bad behavior going. It might not be that you love coffee unconditionally or need it to survive; you might just be used to having it at certain times throughout the day or keeping a cup near you while you work.

Replacing a cup of coffee with a bottle of water allows you to keep up that drinking habit without the ill effects of all the caffeine. Makes sense?

Change Your Order

Psychologists have found that it's useful to employ *if-then* statements when you're about to face a situation where you're trying to change your behavior.

If this situation arises, then I will do this.

If you find yourself in a coffee shop, at a breakfast meeting, at a friend's place with a mug of coffee shoved in your face, have a plan. You could ask for water or a tea instead. Again, it allows you to mindlessly drink something and mimic that coffee-sipping behavior without actually indulging in a caffeine-loaded beverage.

You could also let everyone know you're on a caffeine detox, so they won't offer you anything caffeinated in the first place.

Gradual Weaning

The gradual wean is the easier, slower option for eventually eliminating your caffeine intake. However, it takes a little more willpower to pull off, since you actually get to keep indulging.

If you're going to go down this route, you'll really need a solid plan. It's a good idea to reduce the quantity of caffeine, then reduce the frequency you drink it.

Try changing all your orders from larges to mediums, then mediums to smalls. Then, start giving up one cup per day. If you're having three large cups of coffee right now, change your order to mediums for a few days. Then, start getting smalls. Once your body gets used to the drop, cut out one coffee.

Now, you're down to two smalls per day instead of three larges. Keep going until you've eventually kicked the habit altogether.

The summary of this detox section is basically that: whatever you're trying to rid from your system, you'll be experiencing some pretty annoying, uncomfortable, inconvenient withdrawal symptoms in the process. You already know that.

If those symptoms didn't exist, you'd be done with whatever your poison is already. Unpleasant as they may be, though, **withdrawal symptoms are necessary evils to deal with when trying to get to a healthier, more self-disciplined you**. Without cravings standing in your way, you'll be way more in control of yourself and your life. You can follow the strategies outlined above for ways to deal with your waning willpower during times of detox, but the best thing to do is to just keep your goal in mind.

You wouldn't be doing this detox if you didn't ultimately want to be on the other side of this addiction. You want this. Don't forget that. It's not necessarily now or never, but why not now?

Avoid Temptations (Most of the Time Anyway)

Cleanse Your Environment

Out of sight, out of mind isn't just a saying lazy people use to avoid their responsibilities; it has some scientific merit too.

Several studies on willpower have concluded that **people are actually less likely to be tempted by something if they can't see it**. Those who kept candy in a bowl across the room from them, rather than right next to their work station were less likely to overindulge in the treats than the people who had the bowls at their desk.

Maybe these people were just super lazy and didn't want to get up, but it was also found that those who kept the candy in their desk drawer, instead of out on the desk where they could see it, also didn't indulge as much as the people with candy right there in their eye line.

Even the kids in the marshmallow experiment seemed to inherently know that not looking at the temptation would help. The kids who looked away from the marshmallow, or who closed their eyes, were less likely to give up and just eat the darn thing than the kids who stared directly at the marshmallow.

The message is obvious: **you're less likely to want what isn't there, so make sure what you crave isn't around**.

Yes, this means throwing things out that you may already have bought. It's a waste of money, but that junk wasn't going to do your health any favors anyway. Do a total sweep of your kitchen and any other secret places you're hiding treats, especially if they're in plain sight.

Out of sight is one thing but, if you know they aren't there at all, you'll be even less likely to be tempted to snack. Even if your willpower wanes to a point where you're about to give in, you won't be able to because whatever you want isn't around. "Present you" has to be a jerk to future you.

Tough love, dude!

Keep It Clean

Once you've tossed all the junk from your life, you'll want to keep your environment clean to help you avoid temptation in the future.

It sounds easy but keeping crap out of your eye line isn't necessarily as simple as just not bringing it back into your house. There's a reason the things by the register at most stores are called *impulse buy* items. You don't always plan to buy everything you end up buying at the store, which can lead to a cart full of junk, and a restocking of your cabinet with all the stuff you just threw out.

There are a few strategies you can follow to avoid the impulse to re-junkify your life.

Start Using Meal Plans

Creating a meal plan for the week is one of the best ways to avoid falling back into the slump of eating junk. Most people grab some fast food for lunch because they didn't bring a meal to work or they stop by the drive-thru on their way home because they're running late and don't have a plan for dinner.

Designing a weekly meal plan eliminates the daily "what's for dinner?" confusion and ensures you don't have to stress that self-discipline muscle too hard. If you're at work without a lunch plan, you'll have the option between something healthy and something unhealthy. You'll basically be able to go anywhere and choose anything you want to eat. Deciding on something good for you can be a real strain on your willpower.

If you plan your lunches for the week and take them with you every day, you won't have that problem. It doesn't take a lot of willpower to choose the only option.

Create a Shopping List

Your meal plan will inform your shopping list, so make sure you have a solid plan for the week before you head to the store. Look at each meal and figure out what ingredients you'll need for each.

Make a thorough and complete shopping list of ingredients needed and then buy *only those things*. Don't deviate from your carefully planned shopping list. There is nothing in the store except the stuff on your list. You are getting very sleepy...

OK, I'm not really trying to hypnotize you but, when you convince yourself that there really isn't anything in the store but what you need to buy, you no longer need to exercise that much willpower while shopping. You know you're not going to put that ice cream back once you've picked it up "just to look at it". It's going in the cart, then into your mouth.

Lists will help you with your self-discipline at the store itself, help you make meals so you don't have to stress your willpower during the week, and save you money by eliminating excess food from your kitchen you'd probably just let go bad and throw out anyway.

It's a win-win-win situation all the way!

Take Healthy Snacks

Avoiding the treat-stocked kitchen at the office can be difficult. Easily accessible snacks often throw people off when they're trying to keep their diet on track. Maybe a dieter wouldn't buy himself a donut, but if someone else brought them to the office and they were sitting 10 feet away, he might be more inclined to indulge.

Another common diet pitfall is being in a situation where people normally snack, like the movies. What's a movie without popcorn? What's popcorn without a soda? Oh, you can make that a combo? OK, add some candy in there too.

It's a slippery, buttery slope that chronic snackers can't avoid. They key to beating both snack attack situations is to bring your own. You might still be tempted, but you'll be a lot less likely to indulge in these sneaky treats if you have your own on hand. Just make sure they're healthy snacks.

Bringing your own donuts to work kind of defeats the purpose.

Plan Your Cheat Meals

You know when you're trying to give something up that cravings can get more and more intense until you have to give in or you'll explode.

The bakery starts calling to you and all the cakes grow mouths and start begging you to eat them. That's kind of a creepy thought but that's what it feels like to try to ignore something you're craving. It always looms over you, getting more and more distracting until you just give in.

Then, you feel like a failure, and your self-confidence in your ability to finish the journey takes a real hit. But it doesn't have to be like that! Giving into cravings sometimes can actually help keep you on track. Not only does it get that craving monkey off your back, it can also help on the physiological side.

Eating a calorie deficit for an extended period of time can slow your metabolism. As your body adjusts to having to run on fewer calories it begins to burn fewer calories overall and lowers leptin levels. Leptin (aka the satiety hormone) helps to regulate hunger and balance energy expenditure. Upping your calorie intake temporarily increases leptin, helping with that metabolism boost, and helping to suppress hunger.

Make sure to plan those cheat meals, though. It's dangerous to give in to a strong craving and *then* decide "I guess this is my cheat".

The idea is to control yourself long enough to actually decide to do something, not to have a cheat meal by default because you already indulged. Without a plan, you'll probably end up having cheat meals way more often than you should.

Notice that I keep saying cheat *meal*, not cheat *day.* People often take one whole day a week and kind of just go wild eating and drinking whatever they want. All day.

Considering that losing 1-2 pounds per week requires a 3,500-7,000 calorie deficit and that eating and drinking whatever you want all day can easily rack up thousands of calories, it's actually pretty easy to set yourself back, even if you're an angel the rest of the week.

Plan out your cheat meal in advance and stick to it. It'll prevent you from overeating or binging, and help you keep on track mentally for the rest of the week.

Rewire Your Brain

Just Do It, Consistently

If you do something a lot, it becomes a habit; continue to do it and it turns into a reflex that's almost beyond your control.

I used to do an angry little whistle at my dog when he was making too much noise, barking at nothing. I didn't realize I had conditioned myself to react to any annoying hubbub with the same whistle until I completely involuntarily did it to a group of friends who were being too loud while I was trying to study. I also always reach to turn the bathroom light on when I walk in there, even if it's already on. These are just reflexes. Things I've done so many times that I don't even think about them anymore; they just happen.

While whistling at your friends as though they were your noisy dog isn't necessarily the greatest reflex to have, the process behind it is really useful to grasp. By repeating a behavior, over and over again, I became unable to stop doing it. And that's all you have to do to create new habits. You just have to consistently perform the action until it's totally natural to you. Of course, if it was THAT easy, all the attitudes you would need to reach your dreams would already be habits. That's why we're going to cover some useful tips to help you during the process.

Form One Habit at a Time

If you're kind of a mess of a human being, no offense intended, you may have a lot of things you want to change about yourself. You might need to quit smoking, cut down on alcohol, start working out, start eating well, and start getting enough sleep, just to begin with.

With so many changes planned on the blackboard, it'll be really hard (read: almost impossible) to try and do them all at once. Remember how your willpower can get pretty easily fatigued if you overwork it. Trying to become a non-smoker, moderate drinker, consistent exerciser, healthy eater, and good sleeper all in one day is going to snap your resolve muscle in half.

Pick one habit at a time to change or develop.

Don't think you have to start with the toughest one, either. Experts suggest starting small when you want to tackle changing your habits. Choosing to work on the easier habit will not only get you started on the road to a full life change, it will also help you increase your self-confidence as you come to realize that you own the ability to exercise your willpower and change.

The knowledge that you've done something before is an invaluable tool in continuing a journey. Pick the habit you'll find easiest to alter and go from there.

Be Consistent

As in really, really, really consistent. Don't just do something a few times a week. When you're first launching into a new habit, make sure you're doing it every day, in the same way.

If you want to go to bed at a certain time, then make sure you're actually under the sheets at that time. No excuses. Set a reminder on your phone and get your butt moving when you get the notification; no questions asked. Not just once or twice a week, but every darn day.

If you only want to watch a certain amount of TV or you have planned to have no more than two drinks per night, then make sure you're sticking to it. When you're attempting to create a new habit, there's no room for "exceptions". One day off will snowball faster than you think. Before you know it, you've given up trying to make the habit stick. Not cool.

Be Aware of Your Triggers

Have you ever been going about your day and found yourself, suddenly, inexplicably knee deep in a terrible habit of yours?

You tell yourself you're not going to smoke today, then there's a scene missing and somehow you're out in the alleyway with a cigarette in your hand. How did you get there?

You may have just been the victim of a trigger.

In short, triggers are events that cause other events to happen. Smokers often smoke after a meal, drinkers may have a drink as soon as they get home from work, and sugar-lovers might try to calm themselves with a snack after a stressful event (like a meeting with their boss or a drama-filled phone call from a family member.)

Whatever your bad habit, there's most likely an event or a certain situation that sets it off.

Few people just decide out of nowhere to indulge. Figure out what your trigger is. Being aware of it is the first step in stopping its power over you. The next time you feel the need to smoke/drink/eat junk, look at what happened immediately beforehand. Is it stress related? Situation related?

When you know what it is that sparks the desire, you'll not only be on the lookout for it, you'll also be able to prepare yourself for when the situation arises.

Either replace that bad habit with a good one (like working out when you get home, instead of drinking) or avoid acting on the urge for a few minutes. Do five to ten minutes of deep breathing or meditation after a trigger occurs and you will probably feel the urge getting weaker.

Take Your Time
Old habits die hard and new ones aren't made overnight. Unfortunately. If you're trying to change something and it just isn't working, don't be too hard on yourself and don't just assume the process is never going to work.

Be aware that this might take some time, maybe even a lifetime, and whatever you need to do to ultimately reach your goals is OK. **If you backslide a little, it's OK. You're looking for long-term changes, not quick fixes**.

There's no point in adopting behaviors that aren't sustainable just to reach a goal quicker. This happens with weight loss all the time. People buckle down and turn into health freaks for a few months. They start living in the gym and reduce their portion to the point it could stand on a dollar coin. And yes, it works; they reach their goal within a few months... But they can't keep up their obsessive behavior forever.

They're bound to yield, eventually, and when they do, it leaves the door open to all sorts of abuses. For some, the return back to their old ways may not go down with the expected fireworks and an orgy of what they deprived themselves of. The return may be more insidious.

It may start with skipping a few workouts here and there because they have a life outside the gym. It may be reintroducing a few unhealthy foods they have been missing.

Either way, before they know it, they've gained the weight back (and more) because they weren't living a balanced life they could sustain for more than a short time.

You have to ask yourself whether you want to achieve your goal in a few months, for a few months, or whether you'd rather take it easy and make sustainable changes that will get you to your goal and keep you there for life.

Self-discipline is not a race; positive change is not a contest.

Part VI: Don't Ever Turn Back by Avoiding Those Common Pitfalls

Holidays & Vacations

Ah, holidays, these cheerful times when you're surrounded by family and friends! When you get some time off work, and everyone is drinking and eating everything in sight. There's nothing quite like them.

But for testing your willpower, they also have no equal. Who wants to skip the office Christmas party to go to the gym? Who wants to not eat three servings of stuffing when you could eat three servings of stuffing? Who ignores the swim-up bar at the all-inclusive resort?

You get the picture: holidays and vacations are minefields of temptations that could seriously set you back if you let them. So how do you keep your self-discipline intact when there's so much awesome stuff happening all around you?

Plan Your Indulgences

You're going to indulge during the holiday season and on vacation. Deal with it now.

I don't think anybody's willpower is strong enough to resist all treats at those times of year, and honestly you shouldn't have to. **In the end, life isn't just one huge test of willpower**. You should also be able to enjoy yourself occasionally without feeling guilty about it.

That being said, you don't want to find yourself unexpectedly digging into your fifth slice of pie, no matter how much you're enjoying yourself. To keep on track you'll want to plan those indulgences before you're faced with the temptation.

The day of a party or holiday get-together, make sure you eat healthy filling meals so you're not totally starving when you get there. Also stay hydrated during the day. Dehydration is so often mistaken for hunger, which leads to overindulgence.

Have a plan for what you want to splurge on and honestly stick to it. You'll get all the joy of treating yourself without the guilt or the stomachache.

Super-Size Me, Not!
Another piece of advice to keep in mind is to watch your portion sizes. Fill your plate with mostly good food, and have a spoonful (or two, maybe three) of the less healthy stuff.

Dieticians recommend using at least half your plate for vegetables. As long as you actually eat them and don't just ignore that half of the plate, you should be alright. Just note that sweet potato pie with marshmallows does not count as a vegetable. Alright?

Keep Working Out
The holiday season can be rough on your workout schedule. You're super busy; you don't feel like heading out into the snow (or, if you don't live in cold climes, just any place

without delicious snacks and holiday TV specials), and your gym might even be operating on limited hours.

Vacations are the same. You probably worked your butt off to be able to afford them, and you just want to spend the time unwinding and taking in the sights. But if you want to stay on track to meet your goals, you have to exercise your self-discipline and keep your body moving.

For the holiday season, you may have to move your workout schedule around a little. Working out in the morning before any of the crazy holiday hubbub happens is probably a good bet. Evenings are always jam packed with festive events. You can usually plan for those, but you never know who might drop in after work or what emergency shopping trip you might need to make instead of heading to the gym. Work out in the morning and you'll already be done by the time the hectic holiday events start crowding your evening schedule.

The cool thing about vacations is that you're probably going to be in a new place you can spend all day exploring. You can get a lot of exercise just walking around a new city or taking part in excursions offered by most resorts.

If all else fails, be the weird dude who actually uses the resort gym. You might get strange looks from the tourists in the buffet line for actually working out on vacation, but you'll be the one coming out ahead. If you manage to keep your willpower up during the most decadent time in a person's life, you'll have proven you can be unstoppable.

Dealing with Illness or Injury

In the same manner, illness and injury can really mess with your routine, and throw your attempts at self-discipline right out the window.

Whether you've just got the sniffles or you've seriously hurt yourself, you just don't feel like doing anything when you're not at 100%. Especially little willpower-boosting tasks you wouldn't even want to do if you were feeling great.

Give Yourself a Break

Being sick is OK! It sucks, but it isn't your fault and you have nothing to feel guilty about. Don't sit around beating yourself up for not being able to make it to the gym, not eating right, or otherwise not making progress on your goals.

Give yourself a break and focus on getting better. Plus, pushing yourself to get stuff done, especially a strenuous workout, when your body is basically falling apart won't help you reach your goal any faster. Don't push it. Don't risk it. Chill out with some Netflix. Willpower is a tool for the healthy. You're excused.

Remember Your Goals

If you're totally laid up in bed, with no hope of getting up and being productive, you can at least keep that ultimate goal in mind. Maybe getting up and going to the gym right now will make you toss your cookies all over your trainer, but hopefully you won't be feeling that way forever.

Eventually, you'll be back on top and able to keep your lunch down while you work out. During your illness, though, keep affirming that you will continue to work toward your goal once you've recovered. It's a bump in the road, not the end of the line.

Make a Plan

When you get back to tip-top shape, you might want to dive right back into those healthy habits. First of all, good for you. Not everybody is so dedicated to the process. If you're eager to get back to real life, just keep in mind that you've been less than your best lately and you may not be able to give it your all right off the bat. This is especially true for physical goals.

Trying to run as fast and hard or do the exact same lifting routine as you did before an illness is probably going to lead to overexertion, fatigue, and maybe even cause that illness or injury to come back.

Plan to be a little behind where you were before your setback. Consult a personal trainer at your gym to get a recommendation of how to ease back into your routine after your illness. If you're coming off an injury, make sure to get the all-clear from your doctor and maybe even consult a physiotherapist to make sure you're good to start working out again, and get suggestions for modifications for exercises that may affect the injured area.

The other option is that you'll feel like you lost so much ground while you were sick that you may as well just give up altogether. First, realize that this is a totally normal way to feel. You're not a failure because you'd rather re-break your arm than step foot back in the gym. Plan to not want to do it.

Know that you'll be resisting going to the gym with every fiber of your being. But convince yourself that you're going to go anyway. Sometimes, the biggest hurdle getting back on track after an illness or injury is your mental state. Keep your goals in mind. Remember why you started in the first place and cling to that reason with all your might.

If your own mental fortitude isn't enough, there are still a few things you can do to try and get yourself back on track.

Get a Trainer

If you don't already have a trainer, hiring one can be an excellent way to help keep yourself on a workout schedule. Having an appointment you'll still have to pay for if you cancel is a good way to convince yourself to get your lazy self out the door.

If you had one in the past, start making appointments with them again. You'll probably have cancelled longstanding sessions with your trainer during your illness, but resume where you left when you feel better. Your trainer will also know what to do to ease you back into physical exercise so you don't overexert yourself trying to get back into your routine. That's a lot of motivation. You'll be cancelling an appointment, losing money, and missing out on the opportunity to learn how to get back into exercise if you bail on your session.

Find a Workout Buddy

Again, making appointments is a great way to stick to a goal. Having someone you'll disappoint if you don't show up is a great self-inflicted guilt trip you can use to convince yourself to show up.

Join a running group, ask a buddy to play tennis with you, check out a Crossfit gym, whatever you want. OK, not *whatever.* Stay away from brewery tours and chocolate tastings. You get the picture, though. Moreover, you'll be able to motivate each other and push yourselves to reach the next level.

Do Longer Warm-Ups

If you're going to jump back into your old gym routine by yourself, remember that – even if you're feeling pretty fine – , your body is still recovering. It's still dealing with not having moved the way it wanted to for a few weeks.

What does that imply? Double your usual warm-up time. Your body needs more time to rev up and adjust to physical activity than it did before. It'll let you assess where you are physically; what you can handle and what you can't.

Don't get discouraged if everything seems much harder than before. Your body can adjust faster than you think it can, and you'll be back in shape faster than it feels you will.

Just Do What You Can

In the early days of your recovered life, you may not want to go to the gym at all. Even if you're convincing yourself that you do and you're fully committed to the process of making it a reality, you're still bound to be a little annoyed that you have to even move out of bed, let alone go do a full workout.

In times like these, you just have to do what you can. Tell yourself you'll get to the gym, do an extended warm-up (see above) and then you can go home.

More often than not, you'll want to do more after your warm-up. Coming to the gym for 10 minutes seems like a waste of time, and the pressure of everyone watching you leave after you just got there may be more than enough to get you to stay and do a few more sets before you slink out to your car.

But if you get to the gym, do your warm-up and honestly – deep in your soul – feel like you can't do any more and just have to go home, then go.

Again, it's often your mental state that will be standing in your way, so if it's just your body that isn't cooperating then you're ahead of the game. Give your body a little while longer to recover and it will catch up to your head eventually.

Busy Times at Work

Take Some Me-Time
During super busy periods, you may not have the luxury of time to keep up with all your duties, chores and goals, but you should always make sure you set a special moment aside just for you.

People aren't robots. They can't just do work forever. Everyone needs a little bit of me-time. Make sure it's positive me-time. Many self-discipline issues come from stressful situations. You're stressed, so you go drink at the bar; you're stressed, so you chain smoke two packs a day; you're stressed, so you binge eat, etc.

Taking time away for yourself can help alleviate the stress that leads to your impulses to engage in those stress-fueled indulgences. Even if you can't do the full stress-bust you normally do (full gym session, full meditation session, full whatever session), do take some time for you. Eliminate stress as much as you can to help you avoid the moments you might want to snap and just fall into your unhealthy coping habits.

Conclusion: the Beginning of Your Journey

By now, with everything you've learned, you should have become a true willpower machine! OK, maybe not yet. But you should at least be equipped with enough helpful tools to start on your journey to getting there.

As you'll see, there's still a lot of work to be done, and that work will never really end. **Self-discipline is not a skill you acquire, then stop working on because it will just be there forever.** It's not like riding a bike or learning to read. It's a skill you need to practice consistently and constantly for the rest of your life. This shouldn't be a discouraging thought, though. Practicing willpower on a daily basis shouldn't be a daunting, difficult task. It should be a welcome challenge you embrace with open arms, a daily opportunity to better yourself.

It all comes down to you. At the end of the day, nobody can force you to do anything, and you're not going to do anything you don't really want to do anyway. You might know you should quit smoking and want to, in some abstract way, but if you don't actually have set your mind to it, you won't. No matter how many Surgeon General's warnings or family interventions you're put through, if you don't want it for yourself it isn't going to happen.

That's the amazing thing about strengthening your self-discipline: it's all up to you. Nobody but you can stand in the way of your journey to self-discipline. All you have to do is want it, plan for it, practice it and refuse to give up.

If you want it, it'll happen. Now, go and chase your dreams!

Want to Reach Your Full Potential?

If you feel like getting serious and investing in yourself, check out the "**Real Life Superman**" series; my progressive method to become the very best version of yourself you can be:

Volume I: **the Strength & Conditioning Edition** – Build Muscle, Increase Your Stamina and Become a True War Machine;

Volume II: **the Fighting Edition** – Learn How to Become Tougher, Deadlier and More Fearless;

Volume III: **the Invincible Mind Edition** – Free Your Mind from Its Shackles and Unleash Your Full Potential;

Volume IV: **the Action & Adventure Edition** – Seize Every Opportunity and Make an Adventure of Your Life.

Let's Keep In Touch

Now that this book comes to an end, I'd like to extend a hand to you. I feel like we're somehow connected now. I hope that the content of this guide resonated with you and your past experiences, that you could identify with my journey, my ambitions and setbacks. If that's the case, no matter where you are in life today, we're kindred spirits with yet a lot to share!

That's why I'd like to keep in touch; so we can continue to progress together. We've both embarked on a road that knows no end, a road to perfection that can sometimes get very lonely when no one else around you can relate. We can offer each other that support. We can help each other become better!

Whether you have a question to ask, a comment or suggestion you'd like to make, or if you simply want to tell me about your goals and the progress you've already made, you can reach me:

Via my site: http://reallifesuperman.com

Or my email address: markus@reallifesuperman.com

It'll be my pleasure to help!

Speaking of help, if you have 2 minutes to spare, I'd like to ask for yours. I need your feedback to find out if I'm on the right track. If you could do me a favor and drop a word or two about this book on Amazon, it would mean the world to me!

I thank you in advance and I'll see you soon, my friend.

About the Author

A black belt in Karate, ring-tested kickboxer who also holds a university degree in Psychology, I have to admit I know a thing or two about kicking butt and imposing my will on my foes. However, the real adversary I've always been looking to vanquish – whether in CrossFit competitions, in a race or a fight – has never been anyone else but me.

I believe in the Latin phrase *mens sana in corpore sano* and try to honor that spirit every chance I get by looking for new, more efficient ways to improve myself and reach the next level. Through my trials and errors, I've accumulated a vast wealth of knowledge. Not only on the **quickest means to attain one's physical peak** but also on what it takes to **toughen up mentally and develop a sharp, indestructible mind**.

In this series of books, I intend to share with you everything I've learned in close to 20 years of studying and perfecting my training. It is the next natural step for me: to put into words all that baggage made of sensations, hard-earned habits and unspoken truths; to extract its very essence without holding anything back. And by so doing, not only will I get better, you will as well!

Some of the facts I'll lay out will surprise you, others may come as a shock, but rest assured that they represent the **fastest shortcut to success**. So, if you're ready for the change of a lifetime, let's get started and discover the Superhero who had been hiding inside you all along!

Sincerely,

Markus

43091008R00048

Made in the USA
San Bernardino, CA
14 December 2016